Sponsored by
Marina's Russian
Collection, Inc., USA.

LARISSA SOLOVIOVA
MARINA MARDER

RUSSIAN
MATRYOSHKA

INTERBOOK
Moscow
1993

CONTENS

Title page: matryoshka "Russian Ikon" by S. Pudovkina

The Russian matryoshka (painted wooden dolls nestled into one another) is known far outside Russia and has a history of almost a century.
During this comparatively short space of time it emerged as an all-embracing symbol of Russia, a symbol of Russian folk art.

There are at present several centers for the production and painting of matryoshkas. They include Sergiev Posad near Moscow, the city of Semyonov and the villages of Polkhovsky Maidan and Krutets in the Nizhni Novgorod Region. Other known centers are in the Vyatka, Tver, Mariel and Mordovian areas. The art of matryoshka painting has spread from Russia to the Ukraine and Byelorussia. The art of authors' matryoshkas has seen vigorous development.

The wooden painted doll appeared in Russia in 1890s, the period which saw burgeoning economic and cultural development. It was the time of a growing sense of national identity and interest in Russian culture and art. As part of this general trend a new artistic current called "Russian style" emerged. The so-called Mamontov circle was among the early centers which advocated the revival of Russian culture. It was presided over by Savva Mamontov (1841-1918), a Russian industrialist, patron and connoisseur of arts who had gathered around him a group of outstanding Russian artists including I.E. Repin, M.M. Antokolsky, V.M. Vasnetsov, M.A. Vrubel and others. In his Abramtsevo estate near Moscow Savva Mamontov built art studios where folk craftsmen worked along with professional artists. The enthusiasts who formed the Mamontov circle engaged in education, art and collection with a heavy emphasis on reviving Russian culture, especially the national and folk traditions. Among the items of folk art they collected were peasant toys.

The development of the folk peasant toy was a major area of their efforts. To this end a Children's Education workshop was opened in Moscow which began by making dolls to demonstrate the festive costumes of inhabitants of various *gubernias* and *uyezds* in Russia and were an accurate portrayal of ethnic features of peasant women's dress. It was at this workshop that the idea of a Russian wooden doll was conceived. Sketches were made by S.V. Malyutin (1859-1937), a professional artist and member of the Mamontov circle, an active pioneer of the "Russian style" in art. His matryoshka was a round-faced peasant girl in an embroidered shirt, a *sarafan* (a Russian national dress) and an apron, in a colored kerchief holding a black rooster.

The Russian wooden doll was called matryoshka. The name is not fortuitous. In provincial Russia before 1917 the name Matryona or Matryosha was among the most common female names derived from the Latin root "mater", which means "mother". The name conjured up the image of a staid, sturdy family matron. Subsequently, it became a symbolic name and was specifically applied to describe painted wooden dolls fashioned in such a way that they could be taken apart to reveal smaller dolls fitting into one another. Yet to this day matryoshka remains a symbol of motherhood and fertility. A doll with a numerous off-spring of dolls is a fine metaphor for the oldest symbol of human culture.

The first Russian matryoshka manufactured from the sketches of S.V. Malyutin by V. Zvezdochkin, the best toy-maker of Sergiev Posad, contained eight dolls. A girl with a black rooster contained a boy, which contained a girl again. No two figures were alike with the smallest, eighth, figure portraying a baby tightly wrapped in a diaper.

S.V. Malyutin borrowed the idea of a "take-apart" doll from a Japanese toy which S.I. Mamontov's wife had brought from the Island of Honshu. That figure showed a sage by the name of Fukuruma, a good-natured bald-headed old man, a doll which contained several other figures nestled in one another. The Japanese, incidentally, claim that the first such doll on the Island of Honshu was made by a Russian monk.

Russian craftsmen who had a long tradition of making wooden objects which fitted into each other (for example, Easter eggs) mastered the matryoshka technology with ease. The basic technique of matryoshka-making remains unchanged and it draws on all the turning skills used by Russian folk craftsmen.

The most common kinds of tree used for matryoshkas are lime and birch. The trees chosen are usually cut in early spring, stripped of their bark leaving a few rings to prevent the wood cracking when dried. The logs are arranged in piles with a clearance between them to allow aeration. The logs are kept in the open air for several years. It is essential not to allow the wood to be too dry or not dry enough. Only an experienced master can tell when the material is ready.

The logs are then cut into workpieces for matryoshkas.
Every workpiece passes through as many as 15 turning
operations before being fashioned into a doll.

Fashioning a doll on a turning lathe requires a high degree of skill, an ability to handle a beguilingly small set of tools — a knife and chisels of various length and shape. The first to be made is usually the smallest figures which cannot be taken apart. In the making of the next matryoshka the bottom part is fashioned first. Then it is processed to a necessary height and the top end is removed. After that the upper ring is made on which the top part of the matryoshka will be fitted and then its lower part is made. Then the matryoshka's head is fashioned and enough wood is removed from within the matryoshka's head to slip on the upper ring. All these operations do not involve any measurements, and rely on intuition and require great skill. The upper part of the matryoshka stuck on the lower part dries and tightens the ring so that it sits securely in place. The turning work done, the snow-white wooden doll is thoroughly cleaned, primed with starchy glue to make its surface ideally smooth and to prevent the paint making smudges and then dried. The matryoshka is now ready to be painted.

The pattern of the first Russian matryoshka was poked and it was painted with gouache and covered with varnish by S.V. Malyutin himself. Until the late 1890s matryoshkas were manufactured in the Children's Education workshop in Moscow and after the workshop was closed the show-case and training works in Sergiev Posad near Moscow, an old toy-making center, picked up the tradition. It soon launched commercial production of the toy and developed the type of matryoshka that became known as Sergiev Posad or Zagorsk matryoshka (in 1930 the city was renamed Zagorsk but its old historic name has been recently restored).

1
Girl Wearing a Brown Kerchief

SERGIEV POSAD MATRYOSHKA

The city of Sergiev Posad, situated 73 km (45.5 miles) from Moscow, has grown up around the famous Trinity-St Sergius Monastery. The monk St Sergius of Radonezh founded a small temple lost in the midst of wild forests in 1340. In time it developed into one of the biggest Russian monasteries.

Arts and crafts flourished in the townships and villages surrounding the Monastery. Wooden toys which became known as "Trinity" toys became particularly popular. Legend has it that the first Trinity toy was made by St Sergius of Radonezh himself. He personally presented them as gifts to children. The faithful who streamed to the monastery from all over Russia bought these toys for their children. Even the Tsar's children played with wooden Trinity toys—*poteshnye* (toy) harnesses, *bratinki* (small bowls) and decorated spoons. They were purchased in Sergiev Posad where the Russian tsars went to pray.

Wooden toys portraying a peasant girl in a *kokoshnik* (peasant head-dress), a dancing *muzhik* (peasant man) and overdressed ladies and Hussars have come down to us from the late18th-early 19th centuries. These were veritable wooden sculptures.
Skilfully etched and painted ladies and Hussars were marked by individuality and rang true to life.
The new matryoshka toy which was fashioned on a turning lathe and painted by professional artists got its second lease on life in this old toy-making center which had numerous private workshops which employed skilful hereditary masters.
The art of making and painting matryoshkas flourished in Sergiev Posad in the early decades of the 20th century so powerfully that it set the trend for matryoshka painting in Russia for many years ahead. That period saw the emergence of the main techniques of Sergiev Posad matryoshka painting.
The distinguishing feature of matryoshkas made in Sergiev Posad was its depiction of contemporary life.

Sergiev Posad was a colorful, truly Russian town to which the presence of the Monastery lent a unique character. The huge market place in front of the Monastery was a bustling beehive of activity. A crowd of merchants, monks, pilgrims and artisans was milling around. The first Sergiev Posad matryoshkas portrayed this motley crowd through shape

2
Woman Wearing an Old Russian Kerchief
3
Girl Wearing a Red Polka-Dot Kerchief
4
Boyar Woman
5
The Peoples of Russia
6
Girl Wearing a Red Kerchief
7
Eskimo

and color. They portrayed girls in Russian sarafans carrying baskets, scythes, bunches of flowers, or girls clad in short winter coats and shawls, Old Believer women in their sectarian clothes, a bride and bridegroom holding candles in their hands, a shepherd with a pipe, an old man with a lush beard. Along with females, male characters are frequently the subjects of Sergiev Posad matryoshkas. Sometimes a matryoshka would represent a whole family with numerous children and members of the household. In addition to the matryoshkas which portrayed contemporary human types many matryoshkas were devoted to historical themes which was in keeping with the then prevalent Russian style: the Boyars and their wives, Russian nobility of the 17th century and legendary Russian *bogatyrs* (warriors). Some matryoshkas drew inspiration from Russian literature. For instance, in 1909, to mark the centenary of Gogol's birth a series of matryoshkas celebrated some of his writings (Taras Bulba, Plyushkin, Governor). In 1912, to mark the centenary of the Russian war against Napoleon matryoshkas were put out which portrayed Kutuzov and Napoleon whose figures contained smaller figures of their field commanders. Matryoshkas also borrowed their motives from folk tales and *bylinas* (folk heroic sagas): "Tsar Dodon" and "Princess Swan" of Pushkin's tales, the "The Little Humpbacked Horse" from Yershov's tale of that title and characters from Krylov's fable "The Quartet", to mention only a few. Along with painted decorations some Sergiev Posad matryoshkas featured poker work. Usually, poker work was applied to outline the ornament of the whole doll, its clothes, face, hands, kerchief and hair. Sometimes, the poker pattern was supplemented with a slight tinging of minor decorative details, for instance, a bunch of flowers in matryoshka's hands or the floral design on the kerchief.

The traditional matryoshka was also the subject of some experimenting. Some figures were given the shape of an old Russian helmet or of a cone. But these "innovations" did not find much favor with customers who preferred the traditional matryoshka shape.

Although the early painted matryoshkas made in Sergiev Posad were fairly expensive they quickly won the hearts of grown-ups and children alike. In 1900 a Sergiev Posad matryoshka was featured at the Paris World Exhibition and became internationally known.

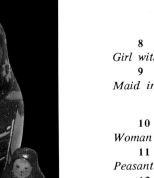

8
Girl with Buckets
9
Maid in a Yellow Blouse

10
Woman with Fish
11
Peasant Maid Wearing a Color Kerchief
12
The Gypsy
13
Woman with a Shawl

In 1904, the Russian craftsmen partnership opened a permanent selling outlet in Paris. It was then that the first foreign order for wooden dolls was made. In 1911 orders for matryoshka toys came from 14 countries. So popular was the Russian matryoshka that enterprising foreigners took to manufacturing *a la Russe* dolls. Such articles appeared in Germany, France and other countries, but the trend petered out because it did not have a national soil.

By contrast the matryoshka industry in Sergiev Posad flourished. The list of products at the Sergiev Zemstvo training workshop in 1911 included 21 types of matryoshkas, each with a distinct decorative pattern. Besides, the matryoshkas were of different sizes and had different numbers of pieces. The Sergiey Posad matryoshkas consisted of between 2 and 24 pieces. The most popular matryoshkas were of 3, 8 and 12 pieces. At a toy exhibition in St Petersburg in 1913, a 48-piece matryoshka made by N. Bulychev was displayed.

In 1910 almost all the local toy-makers in Sergiev Posad formed a partnership called The Cottage Artist. In 1928 it was transformed into the Zagorsk Toy Factory which has survived to this day. In 1918 a Toy Museum was opened in Sergiev Posad which features both Russian and foreign specimens. Among its exhibits was the first Russian matryoshka made by S.V. Malyutin. Soon afterwards a toy research institute was established there. The institute has developed new models of toys, among them a 42-piece matryoshka. The largest matryoshka ever to have been made in Sergiev Posad (the artist Mokeyev, 1967) contained 60 pieces. A Sergiev Posad matryoshka is typically squat; its top part flows smoothly into the thicker lower part; it is painted in gouache and has a varnish surface.

In spite of, or perhaps because of the popularity of the Sergiev Posad matryoshka, matryoshka centers began to spring up in Russia. Usually, these were old centers of folk arts and crafts where turning skills were readily available. Craftsmen were exposed to new ideas in matryoshka-making at fairs, notably the biggest fair held in Nizhni Novgorod. The matryoshkas of Sergiev Posad captured the imagination of hereditary toy-makers of Nizhni Novgorod. Matryoshka-making centers mushroomed in the Nizhni Novgorod Region.

14
The Nun and The Monk
15
The Kulak (Wealthy Peasant)
16
Capitalist General

17
Boyar Man
18
The Gods of World's Religions

19
The Boys of Yaroslavl
20
Mashenka
21
Russian Maid
22
Come Share a Meal with Me

MATRYOSHKA OF NIZHNI NOVGOROD

SEMYONOV MATRYOSHKA

A major center for the manufacture and the painting of matryoshkas in the Nizhni Novgorod Region is the town of Semyonov (which gave its name to a distinct type of matryoshka).

The thick, often impenetrable forests in the Volga area had over the centuries given refuge to Old Believers persecuted by Patriarch Nikon, the *streltsy* (soldiers in regular army in Russia of the 16th-17th centuries) during the time of Peter I and run away serfs.

The old Russian ornamental art was well known in these parts and was applied to decorate various items. This is the birthplace of the famous Khokhloma painting whose ornamental drawings hark back to the Old Russia culture.

The Khokhloma painting preserves the free brushwork which was a feature of old Russian ornament and which contributed to a diversity of composition. The Semyonov matryoshka tradition owes much to the proximity of the Khokhloma center.

Toys were cut from wood in Semyonov from time immemorial. These took the shape of buckets, apples, pears, carafes, etc. Bright decorations were applied with a brush made from the local grass *belous*. The pattern consisted of alternating red and green stripes (as a result the toy was rouged as it were from one side) and covered with light varnish. Painted matryoshkas trace their origin to the time when the son of the famous toy-maker Averyan Vagin from the village of Merinovo, 8 km (5 miles) from Semyonov, brought a wooden

23
Jubilee
24
The Belle of Khokhloma

bell-shaped doll (made in Sergiev Posad) from a fair in Nizhni Novgorod. It was painted with light green vegetable paint (glaze) and it portrayed a muzhik with a painted beard and moustache. The doll was cut in half, like Easter eggs, and this gave rise to a prototype of the future Semyonov matryoshka. The early matryoshkas were painted with Fuchsine (a red aniline dye), then coated with glue which resulted in a darkish hue of the final pattern. Some of the most interesting toys came from the Vagin workshop, for instance, a bald-headed muzhik with a beard and whiskers and stout muzhik in a hat and thick overcoat.

Among other contributors to the Semyonov matryoshkas are the Mayorov toy-making family from the village of Merinovo. Once the head of the family, Arsenty Mayorov, brought an unpainted bell-shaped doll from the Nizhni Novgorod Fair and his elder daughter Lyubov used a quill to apply a drawing and color it with a red dye placing a pink daisy-like flower in the middle and crowning the matryoshka's head with a kokoshnik, an old Russian head-dress.

Gradually a distinct Semyonov type of matryoshka emerged which is more decorative and symbolic than the Sergiev Posad matryoshka. The Semyonov doll is not a character of modern life. Rather, it goes back to the floral ornament of Old Russia. It is painted in aniline dyes with a lot of space left blank and then varnished. First, light touches of the brush mark the outlines of the face, eyes, the lines of the lips and apply color to the cheeks. Then a kerchief is drawn on the matryoshka's

25
Mashenka
26
Good Family Man
27
Lad and Bonny Lass

head, a skirt and apron and the hands. The
focal part of the composition in the
Semyonov matryoshka is the apron which
features a bright bouquet of flowers. It is in
the way the bouquet is drawn that the
decorative techniques of Old Russia can be
discerned. Early Semyonov matryoshkas
were more in the spirit of Old Russia
decorations and the lines were lighter and
more graphic. Over time the bouquet was
suffused with the sap of the grass, and
became more dense, colorful and graphic.
At present, three colors predominate in the
decorations—red, blue and yellow, which
occur in various combinations in the
kerchief, sarafan and apron. The coloristic
solution of the bouquet is the key to the
Semyonov matryoshka. It sets the tone for
the whole color scheme. Traditionally, the
bouquet is arranged on the apron
asymmetrically, a little to the right of
center. The decoration of each Semyonov
matryoshka is original and unique. In
painting a matryoshka the usually female
artist introduces some new ideas. The
matryoshkas from the Volga area bear an
imprint of ancient, age-old folk culture as
interpreted and developed by modern
craftsmen. The turners of Semyonov
developed their own shape of matryoshka
which is more slender than that of Sergiev
Posad. It has a relatively thin top which
widens sharply into a thick bottom. The
famous Semyonov matryoshka is also
remarkable for containing many pieces
(15-18 varicolored dolls). Semyonov also
claims the credit for the biggest
matryoshka ever made, 72 pieces, 0.5 m
(1.5 feet) in diameter and 1 m (3 feet) high.
"Russian Lad" and "Russian Lass" are

original companion pieces. They are more slender compared with the usual Semyonov matryoshkas and are clad in traditional Russian costumes. Instead of the kerchief, the lass wears a kokoshnik and the lad a peaked cap. The pair was conceived as a wedding Russian souvenir, but it ended up as a space souvenir. In 1982 Soviet cosmonauts A. Berezovoi and V. Lebedev gave it to their French crew-mate Jean-Loup Chretien during their joint space flight.

Other well-known Semyonov matryoshkas are "The Russian Woman", "Good Family Man", "Russian Guy". Prior to 1929 the craftsmen fashioned and painted matryoshkas at home. In 1929 the craftsmen of Semyonov and nearby villages formed themselves into a toy-making workshop. Initially it included no more than a score of people. Now the Semyonov Amalgamation for the production of souvenirs is the biggest matryoshka-making center in Russia.

32
Russian Souvenir (Lad)

POLKHOVSKY MAIDAN MATRYOSHKA

Another center for the manufacture and painting of matryoshkas is Polkhovsky Maidan in the Nizhni Novgorod Region. Unlike the Sergiev Posad matryoshkas which were characters from everyday life, the Semyonov matryoshkas which followed the ornamental tradition of Old Russia, the Polkhovsky Maidan matryoshka is a specimen of primitive peasant art reminiscent of children's drawings.

Wood workmanship was an old tradition in the south-west of the Nizhni Novgorod Region. Many of the toys were made on a turning lathe. They included samovars, birds, piggy banks, salt-cellars, apples. It is not surprising that, after Semyonov, the matryoshka appeared in this area. The early matryoshkas, like the Sergiev Posad ones, featured poker work, but then the local craftsmen took to decorating wooden dolls with floral ornaments. Like the craftsmen of Semyonov, they used aniline dyes. The matryoshkas were pasted over, brightly painted before being coated with varnish.

The colors in the matryoshkas of Polkhovsky Maidan are more aggressive and vigorous. Green, blue, yellow, violet and crimson colors contrast with each other conferring a special vitality on the items. Richness of color is achieved by superimposing one layer of dye on another. The decorations are larger than on the Semyonov matryoshka.

The matryoshka of Polkhovsky Maidan is typically a village belle with knitted brows and a face framed in black locks. The ringlets of hair are a genuine element of local women's headgear. The women stuck their hair under the kokoshnik, the maids under ribbons and in their head-dress they stuck black drake's feathers curled like locks. Like the Semyonov craftsmen the artists of

33
Anyuta
34
Woman with a Child
35
Kings and Queens

Polkhovsky Maidan favor a floral design on the apron and omit all other costume details. The main element in the Polkhovsky Maidan matryoshka is a dog-rose with many petals. This flower has always been considered to be a symbol of femininity, love and motherhood. This northern rose is a hallmark of Polkhovsky Maidan compositions. The motif is often elaborated by the addition of rose buds on branches.

Polkhovsky Maidan is at present a large village of about 3,000 people. Young people enthusiastically learn the craft of their parents and carry on their tradition. Any boy of ten can fashion a matryoshka on a turning lathe and any girl of that age can decorate it. Each family has its own way of decorating thus providing variations of the main motif.

In the village of Krutets, not far from Polkhovsky Maidan, the locals also took up woodwork, including matryoshkas. The matryoshkas made in Krutets differ in that they have a greater variety of theme, ornament and interpretation.

The craftsmen of Krutets are given to experimenting. This applies not only to decoration, but also to the form

VYATKA MATRYOSHKA

The people of Vyatka and the surrounding villages have been making toys for a long time. The village of Lugovye engaged in matryoshka painting as early as 1930s. But the Vyatka painted doll acquired particular originality in the 1960s. Straw-inlaid wooden boxes have long been made in that area. The straw used is obtained from a special variety of rye grown on separate plots of land and neatly cut by a scythe by hand.

For decorative effect part of the straw is boiled in a potassium solution until it acquires a golden tinge while part of the straw is left untreated. Then, the straws are cut, pressed and a pattern is stamped on the box. Straws are glued onto raw nitrocellulose varnish. A matryoshka painted with aniline dyes and inlaid with straw is covered with oil lacquer.

Vyatka is the northernmost center for matryoshka-making. Its matryoshka is a blue-eyed northern girl with a gentle bashful smile. It is so charming and welcoming that it claims your attention and attracts one.

The enterprise which produces matryoshkas is called Vyatka amalgamation. The Kirov souvenir factory and the Nolinsk factory form part of this amalgamation. Matryoshka called "Sudarushka" represents a popular style of Nolinsk dolls.

OTHER DECORATION CENTERS

In addition to the widely known centers in Sergiev Posad near Moscow, Semyonov, Polkhovsky Maidan in the Nizhni Novgorod Region and Vyatka, matryoshkas are also produced in Tver, Yoshkar Ola (Mariel Republic), the village of Gavrilovka (Mordovian Republic), on the Urals (Turinsk). The matryoshkas from the other decoration centers have a distinctive shape and decoration pattern.

The matryoshka of Tver is noted for its small size. The decoration uses poker-work outlines. The matryoshka is elongated in form which lends it a certain elegance. They are produced by the arts and crafts and toys production amalgamation. In addition to matryoshkas, it also puts out miniature figures, single and in groups, often inspired by literary works. This accounts for the solution of the Tver matryoshka which also draws on literature. For instance, the matryoshka called "Sister Alyonushka and Brother Ivanushka" is based on a folk Russian tale of that title.

The matryoshkas made in Mariel and Mordovian republics have an ethnic quality. This is true especially of their costumes. Unlike toys from other centers, the decorations are not so bright and rich of texture. It is rather like a geometric ornament. Much of the surface remains unpainted. The Mariel matryoshka, which typically consists of between 4 and 15 pieces is put out by the furniture and toy factory of Yoshkar Ola (Mariel Republic). The matryoshkas wearing Mordovian national costumes are produced in Meltsansk industrial combine in the village of Gavrilovka, Shaigovsky district, Mordovian Republic.

Centers for matryoshka painting have been established in the Ukraine and Byelorussia where toys are executed in a style characteristic of the folk art of these countries. The Ukrainian matryoshka features vivid decorations, the Byelorussian one combines painting and inlaid work.

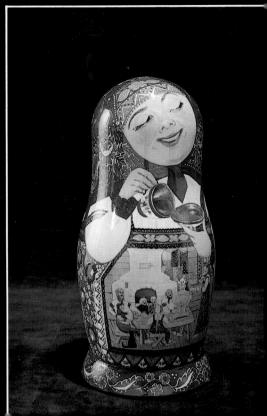

AUTOR'S MATRYOSHKA

The Russian matryoshka is living through a kind of renaissance. Apparently due to the increased worldwide interest in Russia and its economic, social and cultural change. Economic liberalization made it possible for small private workshops to manufacture and decorate Russian wooden dolls. The largest number of such workshops sprang up in and around Moscow where there is a large market for these wares. The biggest demand is not for matryoshkas coming from one of the traditional centers, but matryoshkas made by individual artists, whether professional or amateur.

Modern matryoshka makers turned to the tradition of the early Russian painted matryoshkas which involved professional artists and experienced toy-makers. They came up with variations on the theme of the Russian peasant maid in folk costume which reveal a kinship with the first Russian matryoshka made by S.V. Malyutin.

The fantasy of modern artists knows no bounds. The traditional type of Sergiev Posad matryoshka who usually holds an object in her hands has spawned a variety of matryoshkas representing maids, women of mature and even old age carrying baskets full of fruit, samovars, bast-baskets, all sorts of dippers and pitchers. Their artistic solution is more decorative than representative compared with early specimens of Sergiev Posad matryoshkas. The objects they hold in their hands are like still-lifes.

46
Russian Icon. Detail
47
Playing Cards. Detail
48
A Family Sitting Down to Tea. Detail
49
Palekh Motifs.
50
Girl with a Porcelain Jug. Detail

The classical matryoshka with a numerous family has also received a new lease on life. The mother-matryoshka is often male, a paterfamilias with his family. Having dispensed with the seriousness and pictorial quality of early Sergiev Posad "family" matryoshkas, the modern matryoshka is treated with a shade of humor and at the same time projects a warmth and coziness of large and united family.

Sometimes the painting conveys a gamut of moods, attitudes and emotions. An example in point is a matryoshka portraying a bride and a bridegroom. In contrast to the classical matryoshka of this kind produced in Sergiev Posad in the early 20th century in which the bridegroom and the bride are of almost equal size and are moderately decorative, the contemporary model has made the bridegroom of a smaller stature than his buxom bride which makes a tart comment on the role of the male in modern society. The sly, humorous, sometimes satirical mood of early Sergiev Posad specimens has been convincingly retained in the author's matryoshka.

As before, colorful characters of Gypsies, representatives of various ethnic groups and priests remain popular. Much loved among connoisseurs of Russian folk art is the historical type of matryoshka: the boyar men and maids, representatives of the nobility and the merchant classes in Russia before the 1917 Revolution. The sumptuous and richly decorative dress of the historical characters allow of great decorative variety. Matryoshkas sport old Russian *sarafans* (a Russian national dress), meticulously drawn by the artist with reverence for ethnographic details. In other cases boyar

maids conjure up images of the Russian winter,
fluffy snow, frost-covered trees,
conveying the atmosphere of Russia
as a northern land. In such compositions
the color scheme is more subdued and the artist
sometimes has recourse to the traditional
method of poker work on white wood eking out
the pattern in gold and silver. For additional
effect pieces of mother-of-pearl are used in
modern matryoshka decoration. *Bogatyrs*
(warriors) in mailshirts and helmets, popular in
the early 20th century, have reappeared
in modern designs. The matryoshkas hold up a
mirror as it were to Old Russia,
both pagan and Christian, the traditions in
which its culture is rooted.

A new departure in the Russian
matryoshka draws on the icon-painting
tradition: the Virgin, Jesus Christ and
the Apostles. As a rule, artists
resort to icon-painting techniques in portraying
saints. They treat a matryoshka as a kind of
surface on which they
draw an icon and not as a doll to be clad in the
clothes of a saint.

A hallmark of modern matryoshkas is
its picturesqueness. Often the structure of the
matryoshka doll is neglected to achieve greater
painterly impact.

Attempts to use the matryoshka as a surface
on which the artist positions his images,
be it a fairy-tale or a landscape, go back
to the turn of the century when
the matryoshka industry was emerging.
These timid attempts have provided
a new powerful impetus to the new type of
matryoshka whose wooden shape is used
to reproduce a particular situation. The result is
a blend of two traditions
in matryoshka painting: the topicality
characteristic of Sergiev Posad

52,53
Tsar Nicholas II and His Family. Detail

Tsar Nicholas II and His Family

31

and the decorativeness
that marks the matryoshkas
of Nizhni Novgorod. The apron
is the traditional place for the semantic focus
of the Nizhni Novgorod matryoshka. This is the
feature inherited by modern masters. Several
varieties of matryoshkas can be distinguished
by the way the apron is painted.

In the first variety the matryoshka's
aprons feature architectural monuments. Such
a doll is a souvenir portraying a historical place
of interest. Among the more popular subjects
are the Trinity-St Sergius Monastery,
and old Russian architectural monuments
of Vladimir, Suzdal, Novgorod
and other cities.

Some matryoshkas reproduce the landscapes
of Russia often inspired by famous Russian

55
The Song of Stepan Razin
56
The Song of Stepan Razin. Detail

landscape painters A.K. Savrasov,
V.D. Polenov, I.I. Shishkin, and V.M.
Vasnetsov. But scenes of daily life also form a
major subject. Artists choose landscapes
and stories reflecting the national
characteristics of Russia. Landscapes seek to
convey the peculiar emotional make-up of the
Russian people. This is particularly true of
modern matryoshkas which tell a story.
A notable proponent is Konstantin Vasilyev who
is given to enigmatic images symbolizing
the Great Russia.

  Russian folk tales increasingly provide
the subject of decorations on the front of
matryoshkas. Artists who have
the requisite technical skills reproduce
such scenes drawing on the lacquer miniature
decorative painting of Palekh and realistic
painting of Fedoskino.

57
Folk Musicians.   Detail
58
Folk Musicians

59, 60, 61, 62
Magic Land

There is a growing tendency to use
decorative motives characteristic
of the traditional centers of Russian folk
culture. Some artisans in Semyonov
use Khokhloma painting techniques.
One more and more often encounters
matryoshkas imitative of Gzhel,
Zhostovo and Palekh styles.
The art of contemporary matryoshka
distills the wealth of Russian folk painting
tradition.

The Russian woman remains the favorite
subject of the author's matryoshka.
One might think that there is little one
can add to this traditional image.
But the modern painter succeeds in investing
it with freshness by pressing his imagination
into service.
Of particular interest are the matryoshkas
based on the works of Russian painters
K.S. Petrov-Vodkin and B.M. Kustodiev.
However remote the images created by
our contemporaries may be

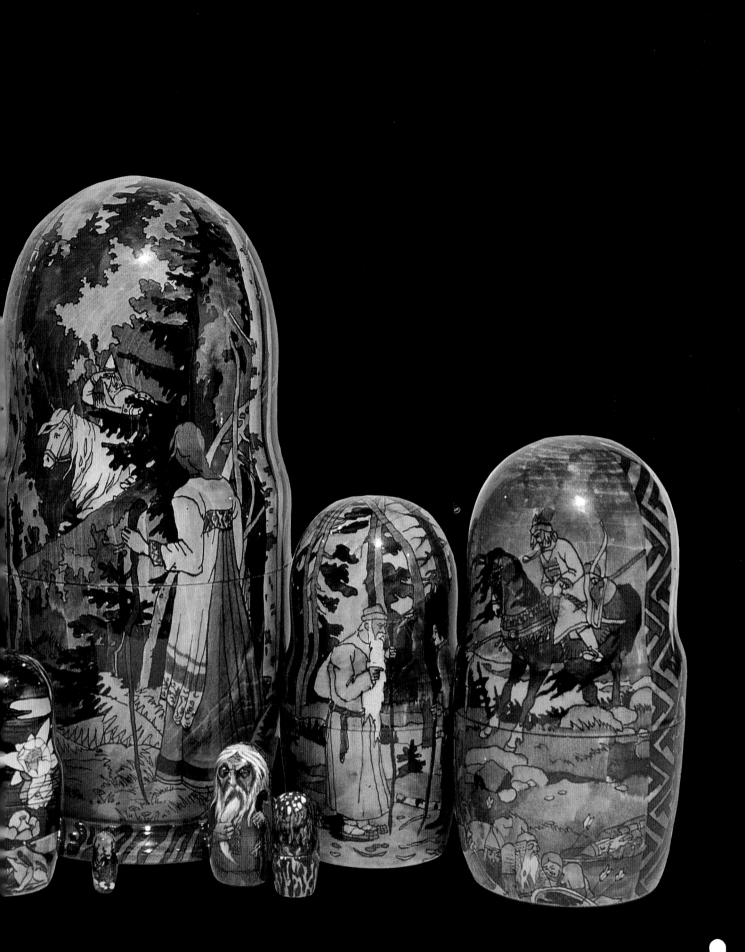

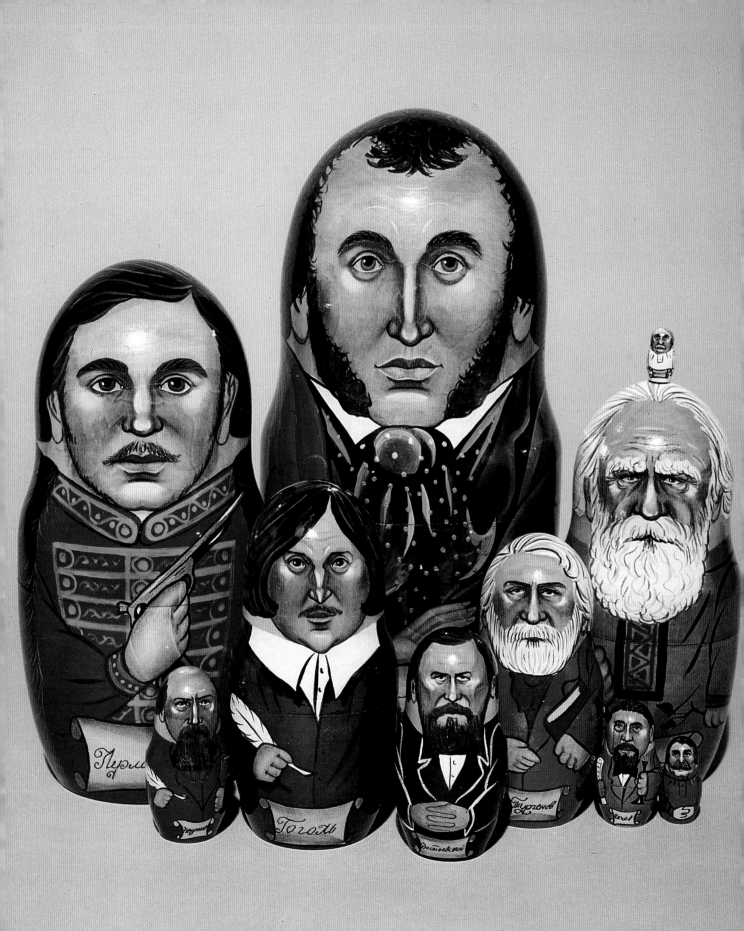

from their classical prototypes, one can discern unmistakable traits of Petrov-Vodkin's Madonna—like women treated as an icon and the full-bosomed, generously endowed merchant-women of Kustodiev. These matryoshkas are generally noted for elegant choice of colors but at times the gamut leaves the impression of lush uninhibited decorativeness. Sometimes artists hit on startling solutions using the tradition of the old centers as a take-off point. For instance, the images of the king and queen pioneered more than a decade ago in the Nizhni Novgorod village of Krutets, inspired an artist to make matryoshkas representing playing cards.

A new phenomenon in Russian matryoshka painting is the political matryoshka showing a gallery of Russian tsars, Russian and foreign statesmen. The painting of matryoshkas portraying modern politicians have a satirical tinge. In this category one can loosely include matryoshkas portraying pop stars and athletes.

The Russian painted matryoshka doll is a unique phenomenon in modern world culture. It is not for nothing that it commands such a lively interest among connoisseurs and collectors of fine arts within and outside of this country. This type of art can be compared with "agitation porcelain" which burgeoned so brilliantly during the revolutionary 1920s in Russia.

Something similar is happening today: matryoshka painting draws on all the freshness and vibrancy associated with the renewal and renascence of society which Russia is witnessing at the end of the 20th century.

65
Russian Writers
66
The Tales of Bilibin. Detail

69
Girl with a Basket Full of Fruit
70
Girl with a Basket Full of Fruit. Detail

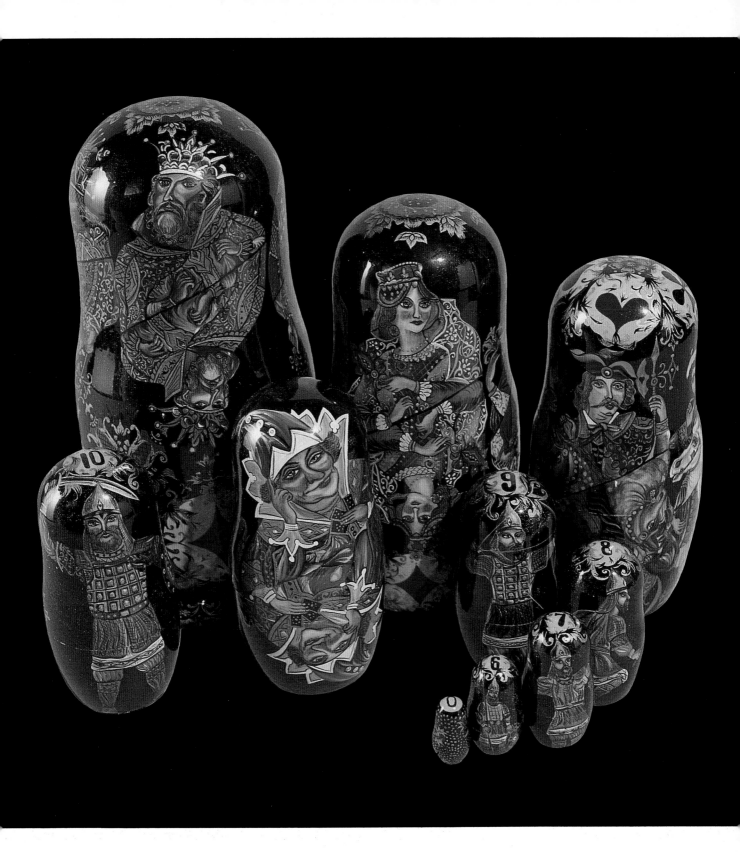

71
Playing Cards

72
The Madonna of Petrov-Vodkin
73
The Madonna of Petrov-Vodkin. Detail

74
The Madonna of Petrov-Vodkin. Detail

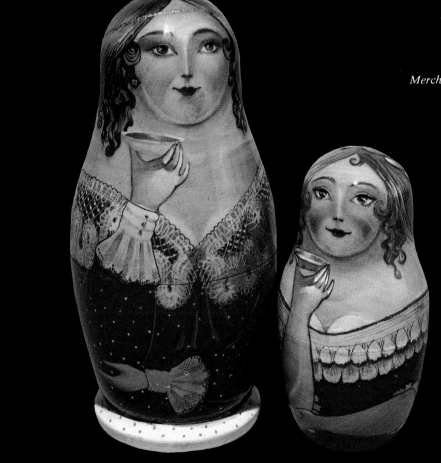

75
Wife of Russian Merchant
76
The Gypsy
77
Merchant's Wife after Kustodiev

81
Girl Wearing a Kerchief. Detail
82
Girl with a Large Bouquet of Flowers. Detail
83
Girl Wearing a Kerchief
84
Girl with a Dipper

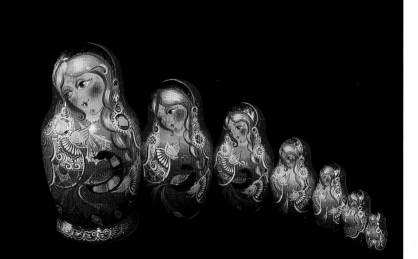

85, 86
Petrushka (Punch and Judy). Detail
87
Petrushka (Punch and Judy)

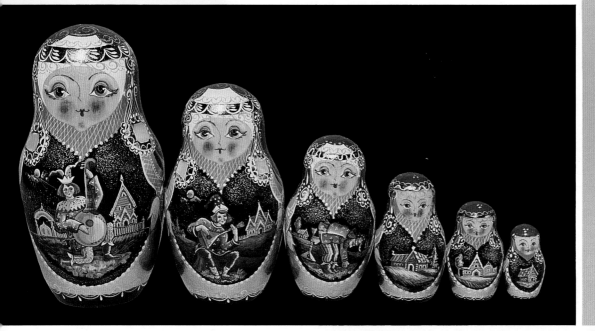

88
An Old Man with a Goose
89
Girl with the Plait

90
Petrushka (Punch and Judy). Detail
91
The Patterns of Gorodets
92
Granny with a Bast-Basket
93
The Tales of Pushkin. Detail

95
A Jolly Family
96
Family

97
Ukrainian Motifs. Detail
98
Ukrainian Man
99
Wedding Party
100
Accordion Player

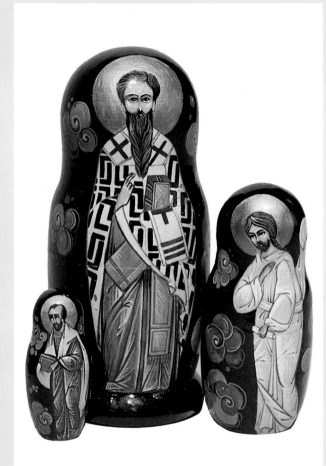

LIST

OF

ILLUSTRATIONS

49
Volynkina A.
14-piece matryoshka
"Palekh Motifs".
Moscow. 1992.

50
Makarova G.
11-piece matryoshka "Girl with a
Porcelain Jug". Detail.
Moscow. 1992.

51
Markevich T.
10-piece matryoshka "The Golden
Ring".
Moscow. 1992.

52,53
Makarov
22-piece matryoshka "Tsar Nicholas II
and His Family". Detail.
Moscow. 1992.

54
Makarov
22-piece matryoshka "Tsar Nicholas II
and His Family".
Moscow. 1992.

55, 56
Volkova M.
11-piece matryoshka "The Song of
Stepan Razin".
Moscow. 1992.

57, 58
Guseva S.
8-piece matryoshka "Folk Musicians".
Moscow. 1992.

59, 60, 61, 62
Guseva S.
12-piece matryoshka "Magic Land".
Moscow. 1992.

63
10-piece matryoshka "Family Sitting
Down to Tea".
Moscow. 1992.

64
10-piece matryoshka "The Tales of
Bilibin".
Moscow. 1992.

65
Viona
10-piece matryoshka "Russian Writers".
Moscow. 1992.

66
10-piece matryoshka "The Tales of
Bilibin".Detail
Moscow. 1992.

67
Lebedeva L.
7-piece matryoshka "Northern Maid".
Moscow. 1992.

68
Zheleznov
8-piece matryoshka "Russian Tsars".
Moscow. 1992.

69, 70
Makarova G.
10-piece matryoshka "Girl with a Basket Full of Fruit".
Moscow. 1992.

71
Buzykin V.
10-piece matryoshka "Playing Cards".
Moscow. 1992.

72, 73, 74
Krylova M.
10-piece matryoshka "The Madonna
of Petrov-Vodkin".
Moscow. 1992.

75
Yermolayeva I.
8-piece matryoshka

"Wife of Russian Merchant".
Moscow. 1992.

76
Yermolayeva I.
13-piece matryoshka "The Gypsy".
Moscow. 1992.

77
Yermolayeva I.
5-piece matryoshka "Merchant's Wife
after Kustodiev".
Moscow. 1992.

78
Marenkova
7-piece matryoshka "Tipsy Monks".
Moscow. 1992.

79
10-piece matryoshka "The Troika of
Mstera".
1992.

80
Ryabchenkova N.
12-piece matryoshka "Girl with a
Large Bouquet of Flowers".
Moscow. 1992.

81
6-piece matryoshka "Girl Wearing a
Kerchief". Detail.
Moscow. 1992.

82
Ryabchenkova N.
12-piece matryoshka "Girl with a
Large Bouquet of Flowers". Detail.
Moscow. 1992.

83
6-piece matryoshka "Girl Wearing a
Kerchief"
Moscow. 1992.

84
Guseva S.
7-piece matryoshka "Girl with a Dipper".
Moscow. 1992.

85, 86, 87
Guseva S.
7-piece matryoshka "Petrushka"
("Punch and Judy").
Moscow. 1992.

88
Gayamov V.
5-piece matryoshka "An Old Man with
a Goose".
Moscow. 1992.

89
6-piece matryoshka "Girl with the
Plait"
1992.

90
Guseva S.
7-piece matryoshka "Petrushka"
("Punch and Judy"). Detail.
Moscow. 1992.

91
Gayamov V.
5-piece matryoshka "The Patterns of
Gorodets".
Moscow. 1992.

92
Gayamov V.
5-piece matryoshka "Granny with a
Bast-Basket".
Moscow. 1992.

93
Budnikova L.
20-piece matryoshka "The Tales of
Pushkin".Detail
Moscow. 1992.

94
8-piece matryoshka "Ukrainian Motifs".
Moscow. 1992.

95
5-piece matryoshka "A Jolly Family".
Moscow. 1992.

96
Zhigareva L.
5-piece matryoshka "Family".
Moscow. 1992.

97
8-piece matryoshka "Ukrainian Motifs". Detail
Moscow. 1992.

98
Mishina Ye.
5-piece matryoshka "Ukrainian Man".
Moscow. 1992.

99
Budnikova L.
5-piece matryoshka "Wedding Party".
Moscow. 1992.

100
Zhigareva L.
5-piece matryoshka "Accordion
Player".
Moscow. 1992.

101
Sinichkin V.
10-piece matryoshka "Russian Tales".
Moscow. 1992.

102
5-piece matryoshka "Girl with a Samo-
var".
Moscow. 1992.

103
6-piece matryoshka "Skomorokh"
("Itinerant Clown").
Moscow. 1992.

104
6-piece matryoshka "Maid with a
Rose".
Moscow. 1992.

105
Ryabchenkova N.
10-piece matryoshka "Girl with
Bouqet of Flowers"
Moscow. 1992.

106
Budnikova L.
5-piece matryoshka "Kolobok".
Moscow. 1992.

107
Budnikova L.
5-piece matryoshka "Pulling Out a
Turnip".
Moscow. 1992.

108
6-piece matryoshka "Girl with
Painted Wooden Dishes".
Moscow. 1992.

109
6-piece matryoshka "Maid with a
Tray".
Moscow. 1992.

110
5-piece matryoshka "Maid with a
Bunch of Red Flowers".
Moscow. 1992.

111
3-piece matryoshka "Russian Saints".
Moscow. 1992.

112
Budnikova L.
5-piece matryoshka "Girl with Pi-
neapple".
Moscow. 1992.

113
Mikhalchuk A.
10-piece matryoshka "Boris Yeltsin".
Moscow. 1992.

This book has been prodused
by Interbook Business,
Interbook Joint Venture.
Starosadski pereulok 7/10, block 5, Moscow, Russia
Phone: (095) 921-39-52, fax: (095) 921-39-20

Director: GENNADY POPOV
Managing director: ALI BAISHEV
Computer composition: TATIANA ANOSOVA
Computer lay-out: KONSTANTIN LAZAREV

The matryoshka dolls are courtesy
of the FOLK ARTS MUSEUM
of the Arts and Crafts Research Institute (Russia)
and the Moscow subdivision
of Marina's Russian Collection, Inc. (USA)

Translation of text in album by JACO Co.,
17 Zubovsky Blvd., Moscow, Russia
Phone: (095) 246-04-02; Fax: (095) 230-24-03

Interbook Business wishes to thank BORIS FEIGIN
for his help in the preparation of this book.